A GIFT FOR:

....

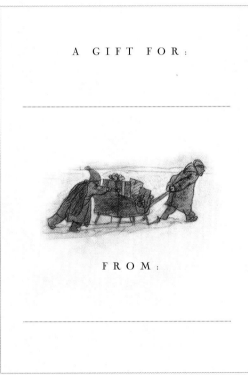

FROM:

....

The Legend of the

Christmas

PRAYER

Brian Morgan

Illustrations by Sergio Martinez

COUNTRYMAN

To Judy
who believed in this little book,
and in me, from the start.
And to those I wrote it for—
the family and friends I love.
May all who read it pause each year
and reflect upon
the Christmas Prayer.

The Legend of the

Christmas

PRAYER

Once upon a Christmas time,
long ago,
a man who had a big heart,
but little money,
dreamt he could give his friends
endless riches.

When he awoke,
the dream kept running
through his mind,
over and over.

Finally, he asked himself:
"If I could give my friends anything,
what would I give?"

He smiled
as he began to think
of all the wondrous things
he could buy for them.

But then he thought:
"I'm a happy man,
yet I have none of those things."

And he began to think
that perhaps real wealth
could not be measured
in riches.

Perhaps there were
gifts of greater value than
the things
money could buy.

In the still of the night,
he pondered these things and
thought of Christmas and what
it meant to him.

Taking out his quill,
he began to write
on a parchment scroll:

My servants shall sing for joy of heart.

Isaiah 65:14

On the first day
of Christmas,

❧

I pray for you joy
in abundance and laughter,
for laughter cures our ills
and joy makes our
spirits soar.

On the second day
of Christmas,

～⚬～

I pray for you
a sigh when you need one,
for a sigh clears the heart
as a cough clears the throat,
and with a sigh
comes acceptance of what
we cannot change.

Let all those rejoice who put their trust in You.

Psalm 5:11

You number my wanderings;
put my tears into Your bottle.

Psalm 56:8

On the third day
of Christmas,

⁓

I pray for you tears when
you need them,
for tears clear the eyes
to see the stars
and cleanse the soul to
let healing begin.

On the fourth day
of Christmas,

❧

I pray for you serenity,
for fights and wars
start in individual breasts
and that is where
they must end.

What does the LORD require of you but to do justly,
to love mercy, and to walk humbly with your God?

Micah 6:8

He who heeds the
word wisely will find good.

Proverbs 16:20

On the fifth day
of Christmas,

⸺∾⦾∽⸺

I pray for you wisdom,
for our priceless gift
is the gift of choice—
and we should use it
well every day,
in word and deed.

On the sixth day
of Christmas,

～∘◦∘～

I pray for you patience,
for most troubles pass
if we wait them out,
and success comes
with persistence.

Rest in the LORD,
and wait patiently for Him.

Psalm 37:7

Be strong and of good courage,
do not fear nor be afraid...for the LORD your God,
He is the One who goes with you.

Deuteronomy 31:6

On the seventh day
of Christmas

❧

I pray for you courage,
for there may be
many pitfalls and dangers
ahead and problems can
only be solved when
they are faced.

On the eighth day
of Christmas

❧

I pray for you compassion,
for we cannot help others
until we understand them,
and we cannot
understand them until we
walk in their shoes.

Execute true justice, show mercy
and compassion everyone to his brother.

Zechariah 7:9

Do you see a man who excels in his work?

He will stand before kings.

Proverbs 22:29

On the ninth day
of Christmas,

I pray for you
a willingness to work,
for work turns dreams
to reality—
whether the dreams are ours
or belong to those
we can help.

On the tenth day
of Christmas

～⚬⚬～

I pray for you
unwavering faith,
for faith shapes our morals
and our destiny
and draws us closer
to God.

The just shall live by his faith.

Habakkuk 2:4

You are my hope, O Lord GOD,

You are my trust.

Psalm 71:5

On the eleventh day
of Christmas,

～⚬～

I pray for you
a mind full of hope,
for hope determines our
attitudes, sets our goals, and
creates our ideals.

On the twelfth day
of Christmas,

~~❦~~

I pray for you
a heart so full of love
that every day
you must give some away
to those whose paths
you cross.

Now abide faith, hope, love, these three;

but the greatest of these is love.

1 Corinthians 13:13

And with each prayer,
the man realized he was not
giving a gift at all,
but hoping that his friends
would find the gifts
they already had within them.

Each time he wrote a prayer,
a marvelous thing happened.

It seemed to him that the prayer,
although offered for his friends,
remained in his heart
and produced in him
the very thing he prayed for them.

52

The man copied his scroll
and sent the Christmas prayer
to special friends,
and that is where the legend
of the Christmas Prayer is lost
in the mists of time.

The man was never
heard of again but, over the years,
the Christmas Prayer
began to appear all over
the world.

People in obscure villages
and big cities would
receive at Christmas time
a copy of the scroll from a friend.

And so the wonder multiplied,
until the story
finally reached you.

May you, too,
feel the warmth and
enjoy the riches of the
Christmas Prayer.